The Country Life Picture Book of
WALES

The Country Life Picture Book of

Wales

Roger Thomas

Country Life Books

frontispiece
Harlech Castle, one of Wales's most strikingly
situated medieval fortresses.

Published by Country Life Books
Holman House, 95 Sheen Road, Richmond upon Thames,
Surrey, TW9 1YJ
and distributed for them by
The Hamlyn Publishing Group Limited
London · New York · Sydney · Toronto
Astronaut House, Feltham, Middlesex, England

First published 1981

ISBN 0 600 36807 6

Set in 12/14 Bembo by
Photocomp Limited, Birmingham
Colour separations made by
Culver Graphics Litho Limited, High Wycombe
Printed in England

Introduction

Allow me to break the conventions of the travel guide by starting on a negative line: as I drove north across the Brecon Beacons a few months ago on my way to the 'Great Welsh Desert' of Mid Wales (a quite inappropriate description in the circumstances), even my spirits began to sink. For a confirmed Welshman to admit to an even momentary lapse of regard for this green, lofty, distinctive corner of Britain is tantamount to heresy. However, I must admit to a suspension – albeit temporary – of affection for this rugged, difficult, beautiful country of mine. I became a doubting Thomas.

There were extenuating circumstances. As I crested the rise of the A470 at Storey Arms, which marks the road's high point before the descent into Brecon, the rain lashed down in a volume matched only by that from a hosepipe on a Hollywood film set. As I splashed my way onwards, the wipers barely able to cope, the surrounding panorama reduced to a mist-shrouded ribbon of waterlogged tarmac, I began to identify with the sodden groups of sheep at the roadside, stoically awaiting the end of this deluge. My spirits began to sink.

I began to feel a sharp nostalgia for the bleached landscape and unremitting sunshine that I had experienced on a recent visit to America. But comparisons are dangerous, especially when based on the privileged impressions of a few weeks in a strange, new country. I did not live in California. I lived in Wales.

The Welsh climate – a meteorological farrago of sun, wind, rain, and snow – can best be described as unpredictable; and in many ways, this shifting, spinning weathervane is a metaphor for the elusive Welsh character.

It is this unpredictability, this capacity to surprise, that makes living in Wales, in the face of the instant allure of countries like the United States, such an attractive, long-term bet. And, as if to prove my point, the weather on my journey north suddenly changed. With the immediacy of an opening curtain, mists receded into clear blue skies. This benign transformation occurred on one of my favourite stretches of road, the roller-coaster B4518 that winds and dips over Plynlimon's empty plateaux north-west of Llanidloes.

As I drove across these mountains, the waters of Llyn Clywedog reservoir on my left, the sun broke through. Birds sprang magically from dripping hedgerows, sheep shook loose their sodden coats, Clywedog's deep waters sparkled in the clear morning light; and across the water, a green burr of conifers along the high ridge of the Hafren Forest marked a delineation between sky and landscape.

Longing for California evaporated with the mists. The road steamed in the heat of the morning sun, drying quickly. I became grateful, once again, that a grim predictability of climate – even one that promises constant sunshine – was not amongst Wales's characteristics. I was even grateful for that first hour of rainwashed gloom, for it had made this present panorama possible, given it a special intensity: the purple outline of Snowdonia's peaks, forty miles to the north, the massive bulk of Cader Idris filling the foreground, the distant shimmer of Cardigan Bay.

But this introduction is beginning to sound like one of my guidebooks, the very thing I aim to avoid. In this introduction, I hope to achieve some insight into the character of a complex country; and in the process, to correct a few oversimplified preconceptions about Wales and the Welsh that are still common currency in those heathen lands east of Offa's Dyke. 'Distinctive' and 'diverse' are two descriptions which crop up regularly on the pages of brochures and travel articles of mine. Normally, they apply to landscape. More fundamentally, they also serve as a collective cornerstone for our culture and heritage.

Unpredictability is our hallmark. Do not for one minute think that flat-capped 'Taffy' is an accurate archetype. Although the vast majority of Wales's 2¾ million inhabitants are happy to be known as Welsh, there is precious little unanimity over the definition of Welshness. A farmer in the rich dairy lands around Carmarthen, perpetuating a family tradition that stretches back centuries, will have an image of Welshness that is significantly different from that of an inhabitant of the South Wales Valleys whose great-grandparents may have left England, Italy or Spain in search of a fortune during the industrial heyday of coal, iron and steel. The hardy hill sheep farmer in the bleak Hiraethog moorlands of North Wales will have his own ideas. So too will the fisherman operating out of Conwy or Port Penrhyn, or the hotelier who relies on a marketable Welsh image. Most important of all, it is worth remembering that nearly three-quarters of the population now live in urban areas close to the capital city, Cardiff, where a concentration of administrative 'white-collar' and industrial employment inevitably results in yet another perspective.

These contemporary divisions in Welsh society are plain for all to see, and contribute in no small measure to the overall picture of diversity. But to understand the many faces of the Welsh character, we have to look further – into the past. The historian Sir Kenneth Dover, when speaking of the Greeks, expressed it perfectly: 'Knowledge of the past plays the same sort of role for a race as it does for an individual. We feed our present community everything we know about our past.'

This principle is as relevant in Aberystwyth as it is in Athens. When we look through the pages of Welsh history we begin to perceive the roots of our current complexity. Our evolution has been moulded by major historical movements – nationalism, invasion, subjugation, religion,

industrialisation – perhaps more so than that of any other part of these ancient islands. Wales has, under a variety of circumstances, been home to Palaeolithic man, Neolithic man, Celt, Roman, ancient Briton, Norman. St David, our patron saint, was in the vanguard of the Christian movement. The turmoil of medieval times left Wales with a legacy of some of Europe's great castles. A Welsh prince founded the Tudor dynasty. And the full force of the industrial revolution, the basis for contemporary Western society, was first felt in the confined spaces of the South Wales Valleys.

Those towering medieval fortresses at locations such as Caernarfon, Conwy and Harlech are undoubtedly our most conspicuous historic leftovers. But they tell only one chapter in the story, for in Wales there is a history lesson over almost every hill, tracing our evolution from caveman to city dweller.

It is a misconception to think that Welsh history begins with the coming of the Celts. They rank as relative newcomers, for evidence of settlement stretches back as far as 12,000 BC. Progress in this cold, inhospitable, distant past was slow. By 2500 BC the climate had improved and a new race of Iberian or Mediterranean stock had settled in Wales. These New Stone Age inhabitants were no savage hunters, for they attempted to control their environment by raising tame animals, cultivating the earth and refining their skills as makers of stone tools. They must, too, have grappled with eschatological concepts for their most striking monument is the cromlech, or burial chamber. Cromlechs – a collection of stones set upright in support of a covering capstone – are to be found in many parts of Wales, notably at the Pentre Ifan site in Dyfed's Preseli Hills and at Llanallgo on Anglesey, where the Lligwy burial chamber is topped by a daunting eighteen-foot (5.5m) capstone.

Wales experienced its Bronze Age, but it was not

until a few centuries BC and the arrival of the Celts, Wales's most famous early settlers, that iron replaced bronze. In addition to a knowledge of iron smelting, the Celts brought with them a Brythonic tongue which forms the basis of the Welsh language of today. They came from parts of England and Brittany and lived a tribal life in fortified hilltop settlements. Perhaps because the roots of the Welsh language, today so important a factor in our national consciousness, can be traced to the Celts, perhaps because we have a deep-seated need for mythology and legend – whatever the reasons, our attitude to the Celts is often shrouded in a romantic, distorting mist. Their jewellery and other artefacts remind us that they had values. But they were also an aggressive race of invaders with a dark, savage side that found horrific expression when their religious leaders, the druids, practised human sacrifice and 'sought the will of the gods by exploring the entrails of man'. And in answer to those who view the Celts as the source of a distinct Welsh temperament, Professor H. J. Fleure (in his article on 'Prehistoric Wales and the Welsh People' in the *Blue Guide to Wales*) has this to say: 'Nothing could be more fallacious than to suppose that a real race-difference separates English and Welsh.'

Whatever its current implications, Celtic supremacy was short-lived, curtailed by the arrival of the Romans. These master empire-builders brought with them their boast '*Veni, vidi, vici*' (I came, I saw, I conquered'). The Romans came and saw in AD 43. Whether they ever conquered Wales is a matter for dispute, for the natives were distinctly unfriendly. This indigenous intransigence plus a difficult terrain thwarted their progress, so much so that their influence was never really felt in the Welsh highland regions. It is evident from the distribution of Roman sites here – at Caerwent, Caerleon, Cardiff, Brecon, Carmarthen and Caernarfon – that their settlements were confined to the less rugged

parts of South and North Wales. Mid Wales seems to have been, in the terminology of modern conflict, a no-go area (a situation which we will see repeated in succeeding eras of Welsh history).

In the first centuries AD, ideas of conquest were reduced to a wary coexistence between Roman soldier and Celtic tribesman. Roman civilisation as we understand it was confined to a few secure showpiece sites at Venta Silurum (Caerwent) and Isca (Caerleon). Today the walls at Caerwent and the well-preserved amphitheatre at Caerleon are two reminders of this partial occupation.

Nevertheless, Roman decline and fall had real impact in Wales. By the mid-fourth century, the Empire was crumbling. The departure of the Romans, in the early fifth century, left Wales unprotected from the Saxons in the east, the Picts in the north and the Irish (Goidels) in the west.

These, the Dark Ages, are shrouded in mystery and legend, a time of Arthurian myth as Saxon battled with Celt. Certain parallels with Roman times emerge, for Wales again became a centre of resistance, the last Celtic stronghold in Britain speaking the old Brythonic tongue. Throughout these belligerent times, this language was evolving into something we can recognise as Welsh as the early poets composed odes in celebration of heroism and valour, invariably in the face of the Saxon enemy.

This antipathy towards the Saxon hordes was complemented by another crucial historic force, Christianity. After achieving a tentative foothold in Britain during Roman times, it spread throughout Wales in the fifth and sixth centuries, cementing the divide between Saxon and Celt, for the former were regarded as barbarians, pagans with alien ways, worshippers of false idols. Pre-eminent during this Age of Saints was Dewi Sant, St David, Wales's patron saint. Today, the stately cathedral at St David's, on the far west of the Dyfed coast,

The red sandstone ridges of the Brecon Beacons, the highest mountains in South Wales.

remains an evocative monument to this religious leader who was born around AD 520.

By the seventh century, Wales was well and truly isolated. New definitions of the opposing sides are now needed, as Anglo-Saxon clashed with Welsh (the old term 'Briton' was by now losing meaning). This division was further reinforced in the eighth century when Offa, King of Mercia, built his incredible earthen dyke which ran the length of the England/Wales border, creating an accepted boundary between the two adversaries. Parts of the dyke can still be seen today, especially around Knighton where sections of this 1,200-year-old earthwork still stand thirty feet (9m) high.

In drawing a line of demarcation, Offa's Dyke brought a period of peace; but only temporarily, for by the ninth century Wales was again under threat from a new seaborne foe, the Viking. For nearly two hundred years these plunderers caused havoc along Wales's shoreline. Today, strange-sounding place names like Skomer, Skokholm and Great Orme remind us of their influence.

When pressed, we sometimes admit (and then perhaps only to ourselves) that we Welsh have a weakness for internal squabbling. The pages of Welsh history seem full of evidence which corroborates this penchant for internecine warfare. Such conditions existed during the Viking invasion, for Wales at that time consisted of a collection of petty princedoms with little political cohesion. Then came Rhodri Mawr, Rhodri the Great. As Wales's first bona fide national hero, he won a convincing victory over the Vikings in Anglesey and united the country politically.

His grandson, Hywel Dda, Howell the Good, bound Wales even closer together by giving the country a universal legal code in place of the previous diversity of tribal laws and customs. Yet Wales's appetite for internal strife survived Hywel: after his death, recidivistic behaviour in the many

Hill sheep farmers are a hardy breed, as are the flocks
under their care. Farmer and sheep have to be tough,
for they are to be found on the windy plateaux and
rugged mountainsides in the Welsh highlands.
Terrain and climate are not their only threats –
today, they also have to face the inexorable advance
of the conifer forest.

small kingdoms, as petty disputes once more surfaced, shattered the veneer of new-found unity. The consequences were far-reaching: Wales remained disunited and weak, England grew strong through unity.

The destiny of both countries, however, was irrevocably altered by a date etched into the memory of every school pupil: 1066. The Norman Conquest redefined England – and added yet another layer of meaning to the already multitiered notion of Welshness. This latest episode in Welsh history again emphasises the futility of looking for simple conclusions in our exploration of this country's character and heritage. For where does our search for a Welsh nation begin? What is our starting point? Those ancient cave dwellers? Those early Celts? Or do we accept the inevitable cross-fertilisation that took place between Roman and Celt as our true starting point? Or was Wales born out of the later struggle between indigenous Briton and Saxon invader? Or the conflict between the Welsh and the invading Normans of six centuries later?

That speculative diversion illustrates, I hope, the pitfalls of national genealogy. Just as with a family tree, the further back one travels, the more complex become the roots. And, of course, there is the added problem of interpreting the past, no better epitomised than by the range of opinions which surround the Normans' invasion. Many Welshmen look upon this invasion as destructive, a further blow to the growth of a separate Welsh nation. Others will take a more sanguine view and regard those tremendous Norman relics – the castles – not as symbols of oppression but as centres from which radiated a new idea of civilisation as towns grew up around the fortifications. If I were pushed off my fence, I would fall on the side of those who see the Wales of today as being more complete, more well-rounded for its diversity of historic experience. To look back nine hundred years and feel a twinge of thwarted nationhood is to be too zealously insular. Our heritage is the sum of our experiences, good and bad.

One of history's many little ironies is that the string of castles constructed by Edward I during his conquest of Wales now serves as an invaluable asset to an industry – tourism – which makes a large contribution to the Welsh economy (around £450 million annually). One of the country's great attractions is the experience it offers in visiting these castles, in seeing such soaring military architecture, in touching the chill dampness of solid medieval stone, in feeling the intimidating sensations that Edward I sought to evoke in the native populace. It is not too difficult to travel back those hundreds of years in time when you stand across the estuary on a clear, fresh morning and watch the early sun light up Conwy's cluster of turrets, walls and fortifications. Or wander through Caerphilly Castle on a winter's day – you will soon forget that this impregnable mass of grey-green stonework is in the middle of a friendly South Wales town.

Wales is described, quite accurately, as a land of castles. One hundred are visitable, most built during medieval times, in numbers that are a testament – yet again – to the strength of the opposition. As with the Romans one thousand years earlier, Wales was no walkover for the Normans. It is a case of history repeating itself to some extent, for the Normans, although they made substantial inroads, could only impose their feudal and manorial systems in the south and east of Wales, leaving the wild heartlands untouched. So throughout these first centuries of Norman invasion, Wales was still a country with its native princes and resilient hill dwellers, preserving to a surprising degree its claims of nationhood and independence. By the beginning of the thirteenth century, this dogged autonomy had become the fuel for a movement which had cruel consequences: the submission of Wales and an end to any thought of independence.

The movement was born in Llywelyn ab Iorwerth's time. This native ruler of Gwynedd, North Wales, was an unusually gifted administrator, tactician and politician. Exploiting a weakness in the current English leadership, he extended his influence to all of Wales, in so doing assuming the title of Llywelyn the Great. He died in 1240. What follows is a crucial and crushing period in Welsh history. His grandson, Llywelyn ap Gruffudd, eventually took upon himself the mantle of leadership and continued to take advantage of a weak English monarch – Henry III – assuming the title 'Prince of Wales'.

The accession of Edward I to the throne changed everything. Edward was strong, determined, a man with a sense of destiny and a vision of greatness – the antithesis of his father Henry. An initial clash between Edward and Llywelyn had ominous, prophetic results: the Treaty of Conwy of 1277, in which the Welsh leader was forced to accept humiliating peace terms. The final scene in these hostilities took place, inauspiciously, in a meadow somewhere near Builth Wells in 1282. Llywelyn had inspired a second, and fatal, uprising against Edward. Again, the English king gained the upper hand and Llywelyn, in one of history's many bizarre random episodes, was killed in an obscure, accidental skirmish by an English trooper completely unaware of his adversary's princely identity.

All hopes of Welsh independence died with Llywelyn ap Gruffudd, Llywelyn the Last. Edward reinforced his hold on Wales through a programme of castle-construction, the most ambitious ever undertaken. His seriousness of intent is still evident in the Wales of today.

Wales subsided into a vacuum. The fourteenth century was a peaceful era, in which the poet Dafydd ap Gwilym wrote not in praise of war and conflict, but in celebration of love and nature. Nevertheless a growing sense of injustice prevailed, which was to explode in a revolt headed by perhaps the most famous and charismatic of all Welsh historical characters, Owain Glyndwr. Owain's rebellion started modestly – a mere territorial dispute with Lord Grey of Ruthin. Soon, it had escalated into a full-scale call for independence, culminating in the declaration of Owain as Prince of Wales and the organisation of parliaments at Machynlleth, Dolgellau and Harlech. But this was a false dawn, for as the English monarch Henry IV gradually won back territories, Owain was forced to retreat. Mercurial to the end, Owain disappeared in 1412, leaving Wales in a state of such abject turmoil that 'green grass grew in the marketplace of Llanrwst'.

As art imitates life, so it is with fiction and fact. No plot-twisting scriptwriter with an eye for the surprise ending is needed here, for it is a matter of fact that a mere seventy years after Owain's defeat a Welshman acceded to the English throne. The crowning of Henry VII, Harri Tudur, at Bosworth Field in 1485 not only initiated the Tudor line; more important for Wales, he was a Welshman, born in Pembroke Castle of an Anglesey family.

Henry's accession can be seen as the concluding episode in Welsh history when viewed as a process of separate development. His victory, although a great psychological boost to the native Welsh, also paved the way for a concerted assimilation and anglicisation of Welsh society. In 1536, Henry's son Henry VIII initiated the Act of Union between England and Wales, which brought Welsh representation in the English parliament. In other ways, too, the Tudor succession meant a break with the past as native traditions were abandoned and monasteries – important centres of cultural life – dissolved. It was a gradual process which continued quietly for centuries, the affairs of Wales never

Terraced housing at Stanleytown in South Wales's Rhondda Fach Valley.

receiving much attention in London's halls of power.

This general disregard eventually provided the background for another movement of historic significance, the Methodist Revival. By the eighteenth century, the Church in Wales had become staunchly conservative and pro-English, increasingly out of touch with the people: fertile ground indeed for those who preached Nonconformity, those who read the Welsh Bible, those who could satisfy the spiritual expectations of a Welsh congregation. The Methodist Revival began in 1761, and as it swept Wales the construction of chapels became a major new growth industry. This religious zeal can still be sensed on a wet Welsh Sunday; though the sober edifice of piety is misleading, as anyone who has lived in a God-fearing Welsh village will know. Otherwise, you have to turn to that unique chronicler of Welsh schizophrenia and obsession, Dylan Thomas. The Rev. Eli Jenkins's father, 'undogcollared because of his little weakness', died 'of drink and agriculture'. Like the rest of the cast in Dylan's *Under Milk Wood*, he was not born in the imagination.

Modern Wales is still assimilating its most recent assault: the force that resides in the white heat of the blast furnace and the dark heart of the coal mine. Man's first serious experiments with industry and technology had their most devastating impact in Wales. In the South Wales Valleys, the coincidence of coal, iron ore and limestone in places such as Merthyr Tydfil transformed tranquil country hamlets into teeming industrial centres.

By the early 1800s, a new society was establishing itself in the winding, narrow valleys. Population increased alarmingly as workers moved in from all parts of Wales and England – and even from overseas. Harsh new environments were created almost overnight, new hardships experienced, new attitudes forged. Canals and railways brought a revolution in transportation and mobility. And as man became a wage-earner, a new political philosophy was germinating. In 1900, Merthyr Tydfil returned Keir Hardie, the first Socialist MP, to Westminster.

I had not planned to cover the history of Wales in quite such scope in this introduction. But as I began writing I realised that more than anything else, more than the effects of random climate, dampening rainstorms and unexpected bursts of sunshine – more than the influence of an undeniably beautiful, forever changing landscape – we Welsh are a product of our past. We have an acute awareness of times gone by – whether we focus on the lot of our grandfathers as they coughed up coal dust or that of our remote ancestors as they battled against Saxon or Norman. Our view of this complex heritage determines, to a large extent, our present attitudes. And it is not really surprising that we cannot all agree on a definitive interpretation of the past: do not forget the one characteristic of ours on which there is, paradoxically, some degree of unanimity – our capacity for internal dissension.

I will not deny the plethora of images in which the spirit of Wales appears synonymous with the emotional release at a rugby game or the pursuit of identity through a rebirth in traditional Welsh culture and language. But I will deny the accuracy of such images. We deserve more than these seductive, easy, stage-managed answers.

If it is any consolation, I know of no contemporary writer who has captured, in an all-embracing sense, the trials and pleasures, the conflicts and the consensus, we all experience in being Welsh. There are, unfortunately, only too many who are blighted by a severe tunnel vision and write from the narrow perspective of a thwarted nationalist, a romantic socialist or a pastoral dreamer.

I was driving to Cardiff recently. The car radio was on. Quite unexpectedly – for it was not that kind of programme – the hymn 'Myfanwy', composed by that outstanding nineteenth-century Merthyr musician Dr Joseph Parry, came through the speakers. It was performed, delicately, gently, by the massed male voices of a local choir. This choir at one time would have consisted exclusively of coal miners. Today, its ranks include doctors, teachers, office staff – and the occasional coal miner. As the choir soared, in full, subtle flight, I choked back a lump in my throat: elation mixed with a terrible sadness. Further down the valley, 'Myfanwy' still playing, I passed the pithead winding gear at Abercynon Colliery. It was painted a ludicrous sky blue, the National Coal Board's gesture, no doubt, towards environmental improvement. I looked across to the row upon row of terraced housing clinging to the valley sides and felt the warmth of community and its unfortunate corollary, a claustrophobic concern for the minutiae of life. 'Myfanwy', a hymn of great beauty, finished. I *understand* it, even though I cannot understand its Welsh lyric. Its strains still lingered in the car as I passed an English road sign daubed with green paint.

I mention these things – the hymn, the change in the choir, the pithead's new coat of paint, the terraces, our lyrical language, our capacity for great beauty and the use of green paint – only because I would hate to leave you with the impression that being Welsh is a simple matter.

Roger Thomas.

William Wordsworth wrote about the Wye Valley's
sylvan beauty in terms which became tourism's first
clichés. The beauty of Tintern Abbey is real enough
though: soaring archways and fine architectural
detail still intact, despite the ravages of time and the
Reformation. The surviving building dates from the
thirteenth century though the abbey was originally
founded in 1131, by Cistercian monks.

Two famous sons of Monmouth. Henry V, born here in 1387, presides in appropriate regal manner over Agincourt Square. For once, a Rolls has to take second place, for the square's other inhabitant is Charles Rolls, co-founder of Rolls-Royce and pioneer aviator (the first to fly the Channel both ways without landing). This attractive borderland town is full of historic connections, another of which is supplied by Admiral Lord Nelson, whose visit in 1802 is commemorated in the local museum.

Guarding the western approaches of Monmouth is the Monnow Bridge, the only remaining fortified bridge gateway in Britain and one of the few in Europe. This thirteenth-century Norman bridge, constructed to control access into a strategic borderland base, still fulfils its role – as any motorist passing under the narrow portal on a busy day will testify.

Chepstow, at the southern approach to
Wye Valley, is a well-known entry poin
Wales. It is evident from its castle (below) t
strategic value has long been appreciated,
fortress was one of the first built in Wales
Normans. Founded just one year after the C
in 1066, the castle was used as a base from
Norman forces advanced into the Welsh kir
of Gwent. The present castle derives from
periods of construction.

The stately, handsome – almost domestic – air of
Raglan Castle (right) reflects architectural motives
that are more social than military. Although
founded in 1067, about the same time as nearby
Chepstow, the castle is largely fifteenth-century in
its present form. More a monument to comfort and
grandeur than to the need for an impregnable
system of defences, it has features such as a buttery,
pantry and state apartments. It is also significant as
the last example of medieval fortification in Britain.
Its great tower and moat must – together with
its home comforts – have helped it endure the
longest siege in the Civil War.

The ruins of Llanthony Priory, in the heart o
Black Mountains. Located in the tranquil Ho
Valley just a stone's throw from the Wales/En
border, Llanthony's substantial remains prob
date from the end of the twelfth century. In a
1100 a somewhat fanciful knight, William de
founded the first religious house in this still-se
spot, and prayed for its immunity from wor
riches.

An early theatre-in-the-round. Its audience, six thousand excited spectators accommodated on wooden seats ranged along the banking, enjoyed a live and violent form of theatre: gladiatorial combat. This is Caerleon's famous Roman Amphitheatre, constructed as part of the headquarters for the Second Augustan Legion during the invasion of Britain in the first century AD. Caerleon – Isca in Roman times – is an important Roman site. In addition to the amphitheatre, there are extensive remains of the legionary fortress and the town has a fine local museum.

A desirable country residence of the late Middle Ages: Tretower Court, near Crickhowell.

A thirteen-arch medieval bridge spans the River Usk at Crickhowell (*top*). This quiet borderland village, in the east of the Brecon Beacons National Park, is a well-located touring centre, close also to the Black Mountains and the Wye.

There is a world of difference between singular and plural. These (*above*) are the Black Mountains on the eastern border of the Brecon Beacons National Park, where a gently undulating landscape creates conditions ideal for pony trekking and walking. The brooding Black Mountain, to the west, is altogether wilder and more intimidating.

The industrial 'Valleys' of South Wales and coal
mining are synonymous. This small, self-contained
area produced vast quantities of coal during the
nineteenth century to satisfy the insatiable hunger
for energy in a new industrial age. Coal mining is
now in decline as the economic base of the Valleys
shifts away from heavy industry. Pithead winding
gear – such as this at Sirhowy near the birthplace of
Nye Bevan – is becoming an increasingly rare sight.

The Monmouthshire and Brecon Canal (*below and right*). Originally constructed for commercial reasons, the canal is now the preserve of holiday craft. It follows an idyllic route through some of the most pastoral stretches in the Brecon Beacons National Park. Good boat-hire centres include Govilon and Gilwern.

Brecon Cathedral, otherwise known as the Priory
Church of St John the Evangelist, has since 1923
been the cathedral of the diocese of Swansea (over
thirty miles away!) and Brecon. Standing on a hill
overlooking narrow streets, it is one of many fine
architectural assets in a market town where there is a
happy, and rare, coexistence of cosmopolitan and
rural influences.

The Welsh lovespoon, skilfully carved from a single
piece of wood, was once a symbol of betrothal and
devotion in rural Wales. Made by the farmer for his
bride-to-be, the spoon usually incorporated an
almost primitive token of fertility in its design,
enough to shock the prim and self-righteous. A
superb collection of such spoons can be seen at the
Brecknock County Museum, Brecon.

This is South Wales at its loneliest – the sharp outline of Carmarthen Fan in the Black Mountain. At 2,632 feet (802m), this high ridge looks out across the wide, empty spaces along the western flank of the 520-square-mile Brecon Beacons National Park. The Black Mountain must always have fired the imagination, for beneath the Fan's escarpment there are two remote lakes – Llyn y Fan Fawr and Llyn y Fan Fach – surrounded by myth and legend.

The Mellte, Hepste and Neath rivers flow through an unexplored part of South Wales that is largely accessible only to the enthusiastic walker. The effort in tracing the courses of these rivers is well worth it, though: this is an area of limestone scenery with narrow wooded gorges, rapids and some of the most beautiful waterfalls in Wales.

This torrent (*below*), on the River Hepste, is typical of the scenery described on the previous page. Close to this stretch are the Scwd-yr-Eira ('The Spout of Snow') falls, popular not only for their beauty but also for their overhang, which allows walkers to pass behind the falling sheet of water with relative immunity.

The same band of limestone that underlies the spectacular series of waterfalls around Ystradfellte eroded into a vast catacomb of caves. This is an area popular with speleologists, though the general public can also enjoy the awesome beauty underground, at the Dan-yr-Ogof Show Caves, Abercraf (*left*). Here at Britain's largest system of show caves, visitors can walk through narrow passageways into huge chambers, and see stalactites and stalagmites which have grown, imperceptibly, over thousands of years.

The dome of Cardiff's City Hall (*below*) is part of a civic centre justly ranked amongst the world's most elegant. Architecture of another and no less striking kind is on display at the castle (*bottom and right*). This nineteenth-century reconstruction, a monument to Victorian wealth and self-confidence, is full of extravagant decoration. It was the home of the third Marquess of Bute, who made his fortune in the capital's coal-exporting heyday.

In the middle of a friendly, unpretentious South Wales town stands one of Europe's great medieval fortresses (*below*). Caerphilly's concentric series of battlements and elaborate system of water defences represent medieval architecture at its most accomplished. Since its founding in 1271 Caerphilly has suffered a number of attacks, culminating in Cromwell's unsuccessful demolition attempt (though he did create the famous 'leaning tower' on the left of the gatehouse!).

Another of the Marquess of Bute's fairytale extravaganzas (*right*). In addition to restoring Cardiff Castle, he commissioned from his hard-working architect William Burges this country residence, Castell Coch, a few miles north of Cardiff. Its location amongst the trees on a steep hillside complements its romantic, decorative design. Not surprisingly, the castle is now popular with film-makers who cannot afford the expense of location work in the Transylvanian Alps.

A room with a view: gilded and painted decoration on the ceiling of Castell Coch's drawing room.

This sculpture of Christ in Majesty by Sir Jacob Epstein (*below*) completely dominates the interior of Llandaff Cathedral, Cardiff. Founded in the twelfth century, the cathedral suffered extensive bomb damage during the Second World War. Epstein's sculpture, in aluminium, was part of an extensive renovation programme. Not surprisingly, its striking modernistic appearance created much controversy when it was unveiled.

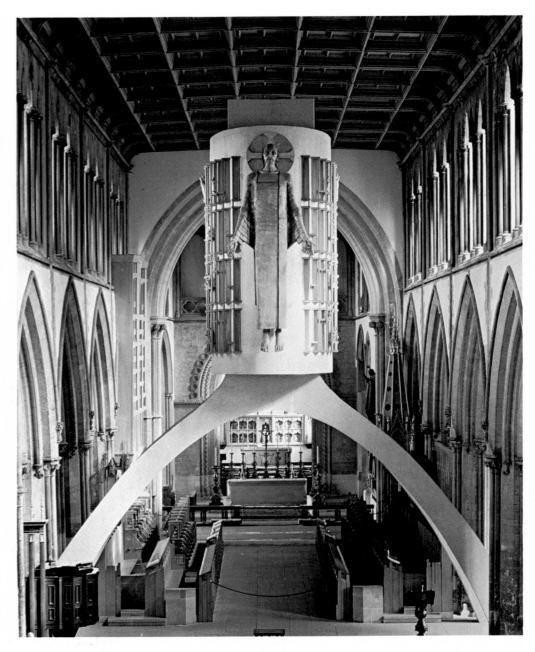

The cathedral's graceful exterior (*right*). This site, in a quiet wooded corner of Cardiff, has witnessed Christian worship for over fourteen centuries. Although renovated, a surprising amount of the cathedral's fine medieval stonework still survives.

Rugby is more than a mere sport in Wales. This game has quasi-religious overtones, especially when Wales is matched against England during the annual round of internationals. If the game has a mystical impact on the national psyche, then its shrine is the National Stadium, better known as Cardiff Arms Park. Competition for tickets at international matches is almost as intense as the battles on the field.

The pretty country village of St Fagans, near
Cardiff, is the home of one of the world's best folk
museums. The term 'museum' is a misnomer, for
the Welsh Folk Museum is a living monument to
the way of life in rural Wales of old. In spacious
parklands, buildings from all parts of Wales – like
this cockpit (*top*) and whitewashed cottage (*above*) –
have been reconstructed, stone by stone, tile by tile.
Visitors can also explore an Elizabethan mansion and
a modern museum block.

Swansea is blessed with one of the best fresh food markets in Wales. Visitors can rub shoulders with the discriminating housewives of south-west Wales and buy the best local produce – everything from succulent Welsh lamb to home-cooked Welshcakes. Above all, there is the seafood, especially the cockles, freshly picked from the nearby Penclawdd beds, and that most famous – or infamous – of Welsh dishes, laverbread, a gooey puréed seaweed that has to taste better than it looks.

A visit to the Welsh Miners Museum near Cymmer
in the Afan Valley serves as a thought-provoking
introduction to the historic coal-mining
communities of South Wales. The museum is
dedicated to describing the heroic – and harsh –
realities of 'coal-getting' in this area during the
nineteenth century. Amongst its exhibits – many of
which were donated by local people – there is a
section of re-created coal mine.

The Mumbles Lighthouse flashes its warning signals at the rocky western extremity of Swansea Bay. Swansea, Wales's second city, has close associations with the sea: it is known, in fact, as 'The City by the Sea'. The Mumbles is a sailing and water-sports centre, popular with those who take to the waves for pleasure. Across the bay there is the other side of the nautical coin – the commercial docklands.

The Mumbles also guards the eastern approach to the Gower Peninsula. The unblemished beauty of its coastline is in no small way due to its protected status as an 'area of outstanding natural beauty', the first part of Britain to be designated as such. Headlands, coves and beaches at Three Cliffs Bay are typical of the rugged coastline along South Gower. The flatter, exposed dunelands and burrows along the northern shore are altogether different in character.

Take one of the windiest walks in Wales to the tip of
Worms Head. Check the tides with the coastguard
at Rhosilli first, though, for this narrow promontory
on the western edge of Gower is connected to the
peninsula by a causeway which is often under water!
Quite magnificent views across to distant
Pembrokeshire are the reward for walkers – on a
clear day.

Many visitors view one of Wales's longest beaches
(*above*) from the air, for Rhosilli's skies are often filled
with hang-gliders. The latter-day Icarus also enjoys
a perspective of the prosperous farms and pretty
village architecture (*top*) of inland Gower.

Lonely Carreg Cennen Castle (*left*) stands, almost
forgotten, on a remote crag overlooking the mass of
the Black Mountain. This, one of Wales's few native
fortresses, has a rare sense of the dramatic, of man's
tentative foothold in wild, inaccessible territory.
Much the same spirit pervades the new Llyn Brianne
Reservoir (*below*), though its construction has
opened up a previously untravelled and untouched
stretch of hill country north of Llandovery.

From his boathouse retreat (*below*) on the edge of
sleepy Laugharne, Dylan Thomas looked out across
the 'heron priested shore' of the Taf and Towy
estuaries; and from the town he drew his inspiration
for *Under Milk Wood*, for it is generally recognised
that fictitious Llareggub has its roots in Laugharne.
Precious little has changed in the town since Dylan's
time, though the boathouse is now a museum
dedicated to the poet's life and works.

On the last Thursday in every month all roads lead
to a most unlikely destination – Llanybydder (*left,
top*), a small market town in the heart of the country
near Lampeter. Horse and pony dealers from all
over Britain – and further afield – converge here at
one of the few places which still hold important
monthly horse fairs.

The powerful, three-storeyed gatehouse at Kidwelly
Castle (*left, bottom*). Yet another symbol of Norman
determination, this well-preserved fortress was
founded in the early days of the Conquest.

St David's Cathedral, founded by Wales's patron saint in the sixth century.

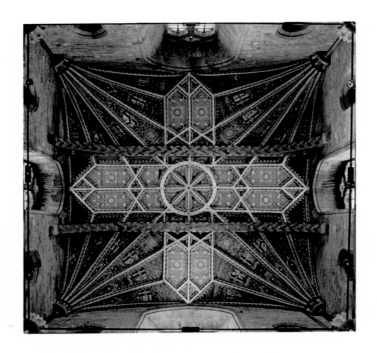

A richly decorated interior at St David's contrasts
with the cathedral's staid exterior. The fine
art of the medieval woodcarver is evident in the
roof of Irish oak and the ornamented tower ceiling
(*above*). Religious art of a different kind can be seen
in Carew's Celtic Cross (*below*), erected around 1035
in memory of a Welsh king.

Huddled beneath towering cliff scenery at St Govan's Head on the southern Dyfed coast is this tiny chapel. Accessible by fifty-two stone steps, the building reminds us of the sometimes reclusive nature of religious devotion. Those who made the effort to visit this site could once recuperate with the help of waters from the chapel's well, which were claimed to have healing powers. There is no such reward today as the well is now dry.

The harbour at Tenby. This attractive resort within
the Pembrokeshire Coast National Park makes few
concessions to its role as a popular seaside holiday
centre. Its Georgian harbour, sandy beaches and
narrow medieval streets remain well insulated
against the garish, unsympathetic developments
which afflict all too many resorts.

The appeal of Dyfed's cliff scenery is evident for miles along the coast, though nowhere more so than at the towering rock formation known as 'The Green Bridge of Wales', west of Tenby. This falls within the confines of the Pembrokeshire Coast National Park, which stretches for over a hundred and sixty miles, from Amroth in the south to Cardigan. These parklands enjoy protected status so that they can be preserved as one of Britain's most unspoilt areas of natural beauty.

The southern shores of St David's peninsula are dotted with tiny inlets and coves, such as this sheltered harbour at Porthclais (*left*). They are best visited on foot by following sections of the long-distance Pembrokeshire Coast footpath.

Laugharne may be the spiritual home of Dylan Thomas's Llareggub (spell it backwards if you want an explanation of its meaning!). Lower Fishguard (*above*) is its representative on celluloid – it was the setting for Dylan's imaginary seaside town in the film of *Under Milk Wood*, which starred Richard Burton and Elizabeth Taylor.

Haunting Pentre Ifan Cromlech (*below*) in Dyfed's Preseli Hills. This ancient burial chamber, one of the finest megalithic monuments in Wales, has clear connections with Stonehenge: both were constructed from Preseli's 'blue stones'. What we see today is the 'skeleton' of the chamber, for it would originally have been covered by an earthen mound.

The Pembrokeshire Coast National Park (*right*) should not be looked upon simply as a holiday playground. The park's motif, the puffin, is a symbol for a protected habitat in which seabirds, flowers and fauna can flourish. It is worth reflecting, whenever one encounters such a spectacular, prolific coastline as this, that a delicate balance exists between conservation and popularisation. Undoubtedly, these are seen by many as strictly non-complementary forces – it is easy to light the blue touchpaper by uttering the incendiary word 'tourism' in certain company.

Most things in Mwnt are in miniature: small
protected cove, half-moon sandy beach, and tiny
whitewashed chapel. The flanking headlands and
hills accentuate the delicate, concentrated beauty of
this off-the-beaten-track part of the Cardigan Bay
coastline west of Aberporth.

The coracle, along with the leek, daffodil and
dragon, is a Welsh cliché. Nevertheless, this unique
Welsh craft, which has been in use since the Iron
Age, can still be seen on the Towy and Teifi rivers.
These precarious-looking boats have changed little
over the centuries – the lightweight frame still
consists of intertwined laths of hazel and willow.
Every August the Teifiside village of Cilgerran
holds an entertaining Coracle Festival.

This delicate Norman archway at Strata Florida Abbey (*below*) frames an evocative, silent ruin. The Cistercian monks who established this abbey in the twelfth century were successful hill sheep farmers, the lonely slopes of Plynlimon providing excellent pasture. This tranquil spot, still surrounded by hill farms, is reputedly the last resting place of Wales's famous romantic poet of the fourteenth century, Dafydd ap Gwilym.

The huge arc in the Mid-Wales coastline is known as Cardigan Bay. All along these mountain-backed shores there are smallish resorts and fishing centres, traditional in style and atmosphere. Aberaeron (*right, top*) is typical, though its harbour lined with elegant, Georgian-style housing is something quite special. Aberystwyth (*right, bottom*), in the middle of the bay, is the 'capital' of Mid Wales, a seaside resort, university town and important administrative centre. Yet its population – a mere twelve thousand – is an index of the fact that 'small is beautiful' in this uncompromising, unchanging part of Wales.

Pony trekking (*right*) is a popular pastime in Wales. The terrain is ideal: hill country, rarely rising above 2,000 feet (600m), which can be explored from top to bottom on horseback. Trekking, it is claimed, was 'invented' here in the late 1950s at Llanwrtyd Wells, an old spa town in the heart of Mid Wales. It has certainly spread since. Today, there are trekking centres in all parts of Wales.

It is water, water everywhere in Mid Wales, especially in the Elan Valley lakelands west of Rhayader. Much of this water finds its way into Birmingham's plumbing system. A series of dams, including the Craig Goch (*above*), was constructed here around the turn of the century. Although at times a source of controversy, these sturdy stone structures and the huge reservoirs that they created have in many ways enhanced a wild Plynlimon landscape. All in all, a series of five dams creates a chain of lakes nine miles long.

Powis Castle, near Welshpool, is one of Wales's most elegant historic houses.

The gardens at Powis complement the castle's air of
grace and style. These formal gardens, with their
terraces and orangery, are essentially the same today
as they were when they were laid out in the
eighteenth century by 'Capability' Brown. The
castle itself, rising above the terraces and the subject
of renewal and improvement over the centuries, has
evolved into an elegant stately home, both inside
and out.

Trelydan Hall, near Welshpool, is an excellent example of the black-and-white timber-framed architecture typical of the Wales/England border regions. This historic building, established centuries ago, is now a comfortable hotel. Residents can see for themselves ancient building techniques, including craftsmen's assembly marks and panels of 'wattle and daub'.

In the eighth century, Offa, King of Mercia, constructed a massive earthwork (*left*) which ran the length of the Wales/England border. The motives of this Saxon leader are still obscure, though the dyke did, unarguably, establish a demarcation line between English and Welsh. Traces still remain, especially around Knighton where sections are very well preserved indeed. Walkers can now follow a long-distance Offa's Dyke footpath along the entire border.

The weaving of wool (*above*) is a traditional skill which can be traced back thousands of years in Welsh history: hardly surprising, with so many sheep about. Many woollen mills still survive; and although they now use modern techniques and machinery, they still produce distinctive Welsh tapestry cloth with its traditional patterns and motifs. It is a process that you can see for yourself, for many workshops welcome visitors.

The timbered market hall in the middle of Llanidloes (*below*). Although something of a traffic hazard, this superb sixteenth-century building is well worth preserving. Its upper storey now houses an interesting local museum.

The source of the Afon Dysynni (*right*) is, like those of most rivers in Wales, prolific: the innumerable streams and lakes created by high precipitation in the Welsh highland regions. In the Dysynni's case, its beginnings can be traced to the foothills of the Cader Idris mountains, the river eventually flowing into Cardigan Bay at sandy, estuarial flatlands north of Tywyn. The Dysynni, like most Welsh rivers, also offers good fishing – especially for the native sewin, better known as brown trout.

Machynlleth (*below*) has a special character, an air of spaciousness untypical of most Welsh country towns. A wide, well-planned main street, ornate clocktower and delicate pastel-shaded Georgian housing combine in pleasant harmony. Yet Machynlleth, for all its individuality, is close to the Welsh soul: here, at the still-surviving Institute buildings, Owain Glyndwr held his Welsh Parliament in 1404.

Lake Vyrnwy (*left*) is possibly the most dramatic and romantic of the Welsh reservoirs, its visual appeal enhanced in no small measure by its Gothic valve-tower. Five miles in length and one mile wide, it is also one of the largest reservoirs in Wales, its water destined for Liverpool. Vyrnwy's claims to pre-eminence continue: located in the foothills of the Aran Mountains, it is also one of Wales's most inaccessible lakes, as anyone who has driven over the Bwlch y Groes mountain pass will agree.

Accessible by narrow mountain road from Arthog
on the banks of the Mawddach Estuary, Llynnau
Cregennen (*below*). This pair of lovely natural lakes,
now National Trust property, nestle beneath the
northern shoulder of Cader Idris. For the faint-
hearted, access by car is far easier (though nowhere
near as stimulating) via Dolgellau.

Cader Idris (*right*) is a formidable mountain range. A
multitude of walks lead to the summit at 2,927 feet
(893m), some relatively undemanding, others for the
experienced hiker only. Cader, 'The Chair of Idris',
has never been treated lightly. Idris, legend has it,
was a giant warrior and poet, any brave soul daring
enough to sleep the night in his chair awaking either
a madman or poet. With its sharp ridges, precipices
and mountain lakes, Cader Idris ranks alongside
Snowdon as one of the most popular peaks in Wales.

The sandy, luxuriant Mawddach Estuary is regarded
as the most beautiful in Wales. This statement is no
guidebook hyperbole, for we have it on good
authority from William Wordsworth, who
described it as a 'sublime estuary' which might
'compare with the finest of Scotland'.

Barmouth, at the head of the Mawddach Estuary, is a busy little resort and fishing centre. This popular seaside town, occupying a narrow strip of land beneath steep, rugged slopes, is an excellent location from which to explore the mountains of Mid and North Wales. Cader Idris rises immediately above the southern shore of the tidal estuary. In its lower altitudes a gentle climate has created a delicious blend of prolific green foliage, sand and sea.

Llyn Tegid, or Bala Lake (*below*), is the largest
natural sheet of water in Wales. Long and thin, it lies
in a fold between the Aran and Arrenig Mountains,
in a resolutely Welsh part of Wales: Bala, at its head,
has deep historic associations with Welsh culture and
traditions. The lake is now popular for sailing and
water sports; though for those who wish to keep
their feet dry there is the narrow-gauge Bala Lake
Railway which runs the entire length of the south
side of the lake.

If you think that the sheep is the archetypal dumb
animal, devoid of intellect and instinct, then visit a
sheepdog trial (*right*). The cunning, recalcitrant
attitudes of the sheep in the face of scurrying
sheepdogs are anything other than 'sheeplike'. In this
battle for authority, the near-mystical relationship
between dog and master is crucial – a twitch of the
shepherd's crook here, a whistle there, and the dog
responds as if by magic. Sheepdog trials are gripping
sporting events, but they also have an important
social side as farmers and shepherds meet old friends.
They are held throughout Wales, mainly during the
summer months.

In the foothills of the Aran Mountains in the south–east corner of the Snowdonia National Park.

The town of Blaenau Ffestiniog merits more than a few brief lines, for this historic slate-producing centre has pioneered a synthesis between old heavy industry and tourism. At Gloddfa Ganol, reputedly 'the largest slate mine in the world', there is now a thriving visitor centre which tells the story of slate mining. And just across the road, visitors can take an underground tramway ride through old workings at the Llechwedd Slate Caverns.

As well as slate mining, Blaenau Ffestiniog is closely associated with the narrow-gauge Festiniog Railway. The line was originally constructed in the 1830s to carry slate from the quarries to the coast at Porthmadog for shipment. Following extensive work by enthusiasts, the line reopened in 1955 from a base at Porthmadog harbour, with the long-term objective of reinstating the route all the way to Blaenau Ffestiniog (the present terminus at Tanygrisiau falls just one mile short of this aim). One of the most scenic of the 'Great Little Trains of Wales' – the collective title for Wales's nine narrow-gauge railways – Festiniog runs through a tremendously varied landscape as it climbs from the coast into the foothills of Snowdonia. Nowadays, of course, the tourist has replaced the block of slate as payload.

Portmeirion is known the world over. This bizarre, eccentric, Italianate (the adjectives can go on for ever!) creation of Sir Clough Williams-Ellis was used as the location for *The Prisoner*, a television series which has assumed cult status worldwide. The setting was perfect, for there is an overpowering sense of displacement at Portmeirion, a tribute to Sir Clough as a conjurer-up of another world, miniature and pastel-shaded, on a wooded peninsula in, of all places, North Wales.

South Stack Lighthouse, on the western tip of the
Isle of Anglesey near Holyhead. The energetic can
follow a waymarked walk which descends 150 feet
(45m) via 350 steps from cliff to lighthouse. En
route, there are nine viewing points which look out
across seabird colonies, coastal flowers and fauna.

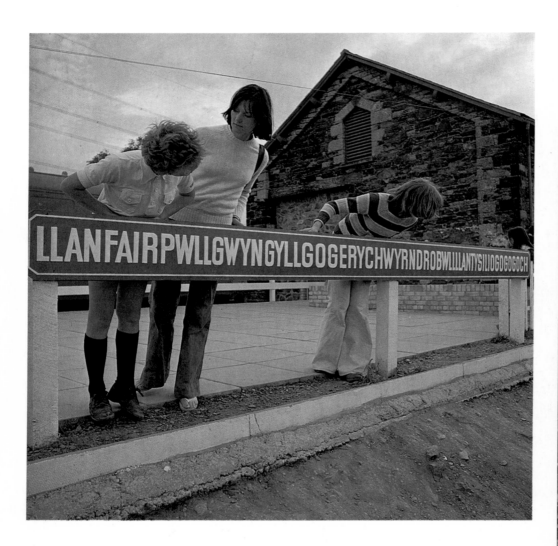

The sign that says it all. One of the world's most prosaic place names, it means 'St Mary's Church in a hollow by the white hazel close to the rapid whirlpool by the red cave of St Tysilio'. Exhausted locals have long since shortened it to 'Llanfair P.G.'

Beaumaris Castle is a paragon of medieval military
design. The last link in a chain of fortresses built by
Edward I in his thirteenth-century onslaught against
Wales, Beaumaris benefited from the experience,
increasing sophistication and refinement of its
builders. This well-preserved fortress is now looked
upon as the most perfectly designed concentric castle
in Britain.

Inside Plas Newydd. This sumptuously appointed
house, now in the care of the National Trust and
open to the public, was given to the Trust by the
Marquess of Anglesey. Its name, 'new house', is a
little misleading – although the existing mansion
dates from the eighteenth century, its history
stretches back five hundred years. Every room is a
citadel of opulence, though particularly outstanding
is the Rex Whistler Room, adorned with the
painter's largest mural.

Plas Newydd's exterior complements its furnishings. In Georgian Gothic style, it stands near Llanfair P.G. on Anglesey, overlooking the Menai Strait and the rugged panorama of Snowdonia's peaks. Style, elegance – and privilege – also characterise the surrounding 169 acres (68ha) of gardens, parks and woodlands.

The Isle of Anglesey is connected to mainland Wales by the Menai Suspension Bridge (*below*), built by Thomas Telford in 1820. This is the world's first iron suspension bridge, with a main span of 579 feet (176m). Still in use today, it has recently been supplemented by a much-needed new bridge across the Menai Strait, the Britannia Road Bridge.

Caernarfon Castle (*right*) is unchallenged as Wales's best-known fortress. Historical purists might draw attention to the considerable restoration work that has taken place here, but no one can deny its imposing, dominating presence as, in the words of one Welshman, 'that most magnificent badge of our subjection'. Edward I, the thirteenth-century monarch intent on subduing Wales, planned that Caernarfon should be the most powerful link in his chain of North Wales castles. With its soaring fortifications and towers, it has an undeniably regal air. The first English Prince of Wales, Edward II, was born here; and in 1969, Caernarfon was the setting for the Investiture of Prince Charles as Prince of Wales.

Aberdaron is out on a limb – quite literally. This
attractive village, on the western tip of the Lleyn
Peninsula (another protected 'area of outstanding
natural beauty'), is the land's end of North Wales.
'The remotest village in Wales', Aberdaron is a
concentrated cluster of houses, cottages and winding
narrow lanes; in direct contrast to the wide open
spaces of its sandy bay, windy headlands and
nearby Porth Neigwl ('Hell's Mouth').

Eisteddfodau, competitive festivals of poetry and
music, are in the forefront of the efforts being made
to secure the survival of traditional Welsh culture
and language. Such events, big and small, are held
throughout the country. The most important,
undoubtedly, is the annual National Eisteddfod.
High points of this week-long festival are
the Chairing and Crowning Ceremonies for the
winning poets who compose in the traditional verse
form known as the 'cynghanedd'.

A museum with a difference: the North Wales Quarrying Museum, at Llanberis, is the former central workshops of the Dinorwic Slate Quarry. When the quarries closed, the workshop buildings were preserved, as closely as possible in their original form, to provide a link with the past. A surprising number of industrial skills flourished in this extensive complex, which houses a foundry used to produce most of the quarry's ironwork, a pattern shop, smithies, a woodworking department and locomotive sheds. The power source for all this is incredible: a giant waterwheel, over fifty feet (15m) in diameter, providing energy by a precarious, Heath Robinson system of belts and pulleys.

The Llanberis Pass, which cuts through some of Snowdonia's most rugged, difficult terrain. Rock-climbing pioneers like Joe Brown and Don Whillans established their reputations on the fearsome slabs and overhangs along the pass. The team that conquered Everest in 1953 trained in this area. So today, it is hardly surprising that the pass is peppered with the brightly coloured anoraks, cagoules and tents of climbers wishing to follow in auspicious footsteps, toe and hand holds.

The easy way to climb Snowdon – on the narrow-gauge railway which runs from Llanberis to the summit.

At 3,560 feet (1,085m), Snowdon is Britain's highest mountain south of the Scottish Highlands. Its austere beauty should be respected, for mists and bad weather can soon descend, turning a challenging walk into a battle for survival. On a clear day the views from its summit (*below*) are superb, extending as far as the Isle of Man and the Irish coast.

Snowdon, viewed here (*right*) from the less intimidating surroundings of Llyn Padarn, gives its name to the surrounding Snowdonia National Park. This huge area of protected mountain and coastline extends south to Machynlleth, east to Bala and the Aran range. Snowdon's Welsh name, Eryri ('The Abode of Eagles'), is an apt image for the entire glaciated spread of these wild, lofty parklands, rich in forests, tumbling rivers, remote lakes, high peaks and rocky screes. But the vision of Snowdonia as one vast pleasure park is blindly indulgent; for all its appeal to visitors, it is first and foremost a working landscape where farmers, foresters and tourists must achieve a formula for peaceful coexistence.

Beddgelert (*below*) is in the centre of some of Snowdonia's most magnificent scenery. This pretty, stone-built village does suffer one handicap: its name, on the basis of a fanciful legend, is translated as 'Gelert's Grave'. The ingredients of this unlikely tale are a case of mistaken infanticide, an evil wolf, an angry king and an innocent victim – the poor hound Gelert. Leaving aside this eighteenth-century potboiler, we can concentrate on the village's more tangible appeal.

Beddgelert stands at the foot of the Nant Gwynant Pass, a road which affords a most spectacular panorama of Snowdon as it climbs to Pen-y-Gwryd. En route, the road passes two lovely lakes, Llyn Dinas (*left, bottom*) and Llyn Gwynant, the former a subject of yet another legend, this time Arthurian in origin. The entire area around Beddgelert (*another view: left, top*) is popular with visitors; and has been for some time, for our ubiquitous nineteenth-century poet William Wordsworth was much impressed with the scenery as he walked from Beddgelert to Snowdon.

The Swallow Falls (*right*), Snowdonia's best-known beauty spot. Here, a few miles west of Betws-y-coed, the Llugwy river tumbles down a rocky series of steps and rapids in a thickly wooded setting. It is best visited in the rainy season.

The black triangle of Tryfan (*left*), the 'three-headed hill' in the Ogwen Valley near Capel Curig. The description 'hill' is misleading: Tryfan is in every sense a mountain, one of the many peaks in the Snowdonia range that present a real challenge to experienced climbers and walkers.

Llyn Ogwen (*below*), at the head of the Nant Ffrancon Pass. Tryfan is one of a series of peaks rising abruptly to over 3,000 feet (900m) from the lakeside: the roll call of mountain summits is so long that Nant Ffrancon in many ways surpasses the better-known area around Snowdon and the Llanberis Pass. Some guidebooks, no doubt written by stout-hearted masochists, say that this area is at its most impressive in rough weather.

The River Lledr (*top*) runs through a picturesque
wooded valley. British Rail have taken advantage of
the effects of natural engineering on the landscape,
for a rail link runs parallel with the river for much of
its route. The railway and the waters of the Lledr
eventually run northwards through the Vale of
Conwy, a rich swathe of farmland and one of the
rare interruptions in Snowdonia's otherwise
inhospitable landscape. Rowen (*above*) is typical of
the string of villages along the vale's sheltered
western slopes.

The Carneddau is a collective name for Wales's
second highest mountain range. Rising above the
eastern flank of the Nant Ffrancon Pass is a dramatic
cross-shaped plateau which peaks at Carnedd
Dafydd and Carnedd Llywelyn, the latter almost as
high as Snowdon. They are said to be named after
brother princes who defended an independent
North Wales against the forces of Edward I in the
thirteenth century.

From the sublime to the ridiculous. Just a stone's throw from magnificent Conwy Castle (*below*) there is the 'smallest house in Britain' (*bottom*). Conwy, more than any other Welsh castle, preserves the air and spirit of those troubled medieval times. Its rugged masonry, extensive town walls and imposing defences have an authenticity few other castles can match. Inevitably, it was the work of Edward I, who would have scorned the miniature vision of those who built the 'smallest house'.

Llandudno, 'Queen of the Welsh Resorts', still
displays that Edwardian elegance to which it was
originally dedicated. Its setting, framed between
the headlands of the Great and Little Orme, is as
harmonious as the uniformity of hotel architecture
lining the promenade; as it should be, for
Llandudno, developed from 1850 as one of Britain's
pioneer resorts, is a product of careful town
planning. More important, Llandudno (like Tenby
in the south) has successfully eschewed the
decorative crudities that often accompany mass
tourism, even though it offers the largest selection of
hotels in Wales.

Ruthin (*left*), in the borderland Vale of Clwyd, is a distinguished little town which proudly proclaims its medieval character, visibly and audibly. The visual evidence is everywhere: half-timbered shops and houses, fourteenth-century church with delicately carved panels, so many architectural artefacts of the artisan and craftsman. The curfew is rung here, too, a custom that stretches back to the eleventh century. And if that were not enough, the town holds 'medieval days' in the summer months, whilst nightly entertainment takes the form of medieval banquets, held throughout the year in Ruthin Castle.

The highest waterfall in Wales (*below*). Pistyll Rhaeadr, in remote borderlands north of Llanfyllin, plunges some 240 feet (73m) by a series of gushing leaps. It is one of the 'Seven Wonders of Wales'.

The waters of Pistyll Rhaeadr have their source in the Berwyn Mountains (*above and top*). Rounded hills rise to exposed high moorland dotted with cwms in this, one of Wales's most remote and inaccessible upland regions. The Berwyns are also one of the country's principal mountain ranges, extending for some twenty miles in the borderlands south of Llangollen.

Near Llangollen the English plains suddenly rise into high Welsh hill country.

A world-famous little town. Llangollen is the home
each year of the International Eisteddfod, a colourful
festival of music and dance that attracts participants
from over thirty nations. Standing beside the River
Dee (its fourteenth-century bridge another of the
'Seven Wonders'), this gateway to North Wales is
an excellent touring centre. One eighteenth-century
visitor remarked that the Vale of Llangollen was an
ideal place in which to discover 'the mysteries of
natural scenery'.

The Llangollen Canal, a section of the Shropshire
Union Canal which enters Wales at Chirk, is one of
the most spectacular stretches of inland waterway in
Britain – especially when it crosses the Dee Valley
on the Pontcysyllte Aqueduct, an eighteenth-
century engineering masterpiece designed by
Thomas Telford. Those without a head for heights
will no doubt prefer the green borderland scenery
beside its banks. Holiday cruisers are easy to hire
(and steer), and there is an excellent award-winning
Canal Exhibition Centre at Llangollen.

Plas Newydd (*below*), home of the eccentric 'Ladies of Llangollen'. Lady Eleanor Butler and the Hon. Sarah Ponsonby were possibly a little ahead of their time. These two unmarried women lived together here in the late eighteenth century, though their professed devotions were to 'friendship, celibacy, and the knitting of blue stockings'. They leave a decorated – some say overdecorated – house which was a tourist attraction even in their day.

Near Llangollen, the ruins of Valle Crucis Abbey (*right, top*), another religious house founded by the Cistercians. It dates from 1201, though extensive restorations were carried out following a fire in the late thirteenth century.

The remnants of thirteenth-century Castell Dinas Brân (*right, bottom*) command panoptic views of Llangollen and the vale. Perched on a steep conical hill, it was made impregnable as much by its location as by its defences. Wordsworth called it a 'relic of kings, wreck of forgotten wars'.

The restoration of Erddig, a seventeenth-century house near Wrexham, was one of the National Trust's most ambitious undertakings. This State Bed (*left*), although magnificent, is not really representative of Erddig's main fascination as a country house dedicated to the old 'upstairs, downstairs' life.

Elihu Yale (1649-1721), benefactor of Yale University, is buried in Wrexham (*right, top*).

Although founded in medieval times by Edward I, Chirk Castle (*right, bottom*) has developed over the ages into a mansion of great style. Acquired by Sir Thomas Myddleton in 1595, the castle is rich in historical associations from many periods.

The nineteen-arch Pontcysyllte Aqueduct (*below*), one of Thomas Telford's great engineering achievements, was built between 1795 and 1805 and carries canal boats in a cast-iron trough for over 1,000 feet (300m) across the Dee on their way to Llangollen.

Born in America, in Europe bred,
In Africa travell'd, and in Asia wed.
Where long he liv'd and thriv'd; in London dead.
Much good, some ill, he did; so hope all's even,
And that his soul thro' mercy's gone to Heaven.
You that survive and read this tale, take care,
For this most certain exit to prepare:
Where blest in peace, the actions of the just
Smell sweet, and blossom in the silent dust.

Acknowledgements

The photographs were kindly provided by:
John Bethell, St Albans 20, 21, 22, 24-25, 36 bottom, 39, 40-41,
54 bottom, 58 bottom, 74, 83, 94, 94-95, 96-97, 97, 116 bottom,
125 top, 125 bottom, 126 top, 127 top; British Tourist Authority,
London 10-11, 67, 84-85, 91, 102, 114 top; Michael Dent, Richmond
28-29, 85; Jack Farley, Gloucester 18-19, 43, 48, 49, 70, 77, 102-103;
Marion Farley, Gloucester 26 top, 26-27; George Hall, Bickley 62, 82;
Peter Murphy, Dolgellau 44-45, 90-91; Hugh Newbury,
Twickenham 64-65; Tony Stone Associates, London 8-9, 56-57,
72-73, 78-79, 81, 104-105, 106-107, 109; Bob and Sheila Thomlinson,
Carlisle 2, 45 bottom, 51, 58 top, 59, 63, 68, 69 bottom, 75, 78, 92, 93,
99, 111 top, 111 bottom, 112 top, 112 bottom, 114 bottom, 124,
126 bottom, 127 bottom; Judy Todd, London 18, 26 bottom, 32-33,
35, 50, 88-89, 108 top, 108 bottom, 110, 119 top, 119 bottom,
120-121, 122, 123; Jason Welchman, London 106, 112-113; Wales
Tourist Board, Cardiff 14-15, 17, 23, 29, 30, 31, 33, 34-35, 36 top,
36-37, 38, 42, 45 top, 46-47, 47, 50-51, 52, 53, 54 top, 55, 60, 61, 64,
66-67, 69 top, 71, 76, 80-81, 86, 87, 98, 100, 101, 115, 116 top, 116-117,
118 top, 118 bottom.